Tomorrow's Waves

A poetry collection

Julia Kellogg Henry

Julia Kellogg Henry

Tomorrow's Waves

ISBN: 978-0-578-92500-4 (paperback)

Edited by Stefanie Briar

Cover art by @agirlwithabrush on Instagram

Dedicated to—

my wave teacher

Julia Kellogg Henry

Dear Reader,

I may not have lived through the same pain you have,
you may not have lived through mine—
but you got here,
and that's all that matters.

Your heart has a place among these pages;
you are welcomed with open arms.

I hope this book helps you the way writing it helped me.
I hope you find some sort of peace,

in understanding the waves.

TOMORROWS

Waves

Julia Kellogg Henry

Thank you to the ones that led me to the ocean
but didn't let me get swept away—

you are my soul keepers.

He always told me to move forward,
to not look back.

But the objects in my rear view mirror
are essential to my journey.

I'm trying to enjoy the ride,
to live in the present,

but I can't help but reminisce,
I can't help but dream.

I've spent a lot of my life being lost,
but aren't those the best adventures?

I have had many highs and lows in my life.
Neither stays long enough
to be *familiar*.

Like a fragile mosaic
set too precariously to the side,
—I shattered.

It took years to put myself back together
one piece at a time;
like a puzzle strewn out across a table
with no instructions.

There are still pieces I haven't found,
ones that went missing so long ago
that I forgot what I'm even looking for.

But maybe we don't need to be whole
to be complete.

Maybe the fact that we are all
a little bit unfinished
is what makes us so alluring—
so *human*.

I'm sorry to all the poems
I've left in bookstores.

I'm sorry to every life changing story
trapped inside a binding I didn't reach for
because I judged the book by the cover.

I'm sorry to all the advice I missed
because I wasn't listening closely enough,
and to all the questions I didn't ask
because I assumed I already knew the answer.

I'm sorry to everything I looked at
but didn't truly *see*.

I used to think that when we died
we became fairies of the sky.
That we got to paint the sunsets
and control the tides,
and at night
when we were done sprinkling wildflower seeds
and singing with the birds,
we would go home to our star in the sky—
and rest peacefully.

I never told anyone my theory,
and perhaps I learned it from a Disney movie
or old bedtime stories,
but I always had a sense that the stars were watching us.

That some sunsets were painted just for me,
as if I was the only one in the whole world watching.
"I see you," I would whisper to no one,
hoping the wind would keep my message safe
long enough for it to be delivered
to everyone that has ever felt forgotten.

And on those rare nights
when it was dark enough to see the whole universe,
I would ask each star who they were,
if they ever got to become
who they always wanted to be.

And I would listen to the whispers as they would answer
with the wisdom the universe keeps locked away
in the darkness between all the light.

I will never understand what it feels like to be you.

I do not know what fills your pages,
what keeps you up at night,
or what you think when you look in a mirror.

I will never be able to comprehend your pain,
or fight your daily battles.

I have not walked your journey
or loved with your heart.

This is why I choose to be kind;
Because that is what I'd want from you
given my story.

Some say you die twice—
once when your heart stops beating,
and again when no one on earth remembers your name.

The second kind of death
always seemed more tragic to me.

I don't fear the end,
but I do fear oblivion.

I guess being a poet
is a side effect of desperately not wanting
to be *forgotten*.

If you ask me where I'm going
the answer is simple—
to see the world.

All I have is a dream,
but darling,
sometimes
that's *plenty*.

I find comfort in the fact
that everyone on this earth dreams to the same moon.

It doesn't matter what corner of the world you are in,
we are all staring at the same sky.

And somehow
that doesn't make you feel as far away.

There is a heartbreaking realization
that all empaths face
the moment they realize
they can't fix the world.

It's debilitating to learn that sometimes
you just have to watch
the people you love as they are hurting.

That it is not possible
to reach into someones heart
and take away all their pain.

Being vulnerable
is not a weakness.

It takes tremendous bravery to be real;
to give yourself permission
to feel life in the deepest way.

Being vulnerable
means having the strength to not always be strong,
and having the courage to show the world
that that's *okay*.

I grew up in a house
that was always on the verge of collapsing,
Where tensions were so high,
the tiniest movement could start a wildfire.

I learned the difference between the words
"house" and "home" very early.

"Home" is a *feeling*,
but it is in no way connected
to a roof and some walls.

Run as fast as you can
for as long as your heart will let you.
It doesn't matter where,
as long as you feel the wind against your skin,
as long as you leave everything that feels safe
behind you—
and never look back.

You have caused oceans of tears
to pour from the very eyes
everyone says I got from you.

After the vines
that were tightly wrapped
around my neck
finally loosened,
I made a vow
to never take breathing
for granted again.

She was so excited about life. Every day was to be celebrated, for this was the most colorful of worlds. She was hardly afraid of anything, spiders maybe. She was different then, she didn't care what other people thought, that was just a waste of time. The world was waiting to meet her, and boy, was she eager to meet the world.

And then something happened. Stopped her childhood in its tracks, and the girl ran away.

A divorce.

A long, nasty, painful divorce of broken promises. One house became two, became a constant back and forth, a million goodbyes every week. Everything was suddenly a 50/50 split and she lived out of a duffel bag.

As winter came the crumbling family shivered with each truth that was set free. Friends turned out to be bullies, love was scarce, and slowly, as her world collapsed, she shattered from the inside out. And the colors in her heart were replaced with black and white.

For 365 nights she cried herself to sleep. It was always the same: frozen pizza and reality TV, the screaming and the slamming doors.
She absorbed every name he called her until she hated herself.

People kept saying everything was going to be ok, but she stopped believing them. How empty those words become when they get overused. He's a good man they would say. He's just heartbroken, you have to love him they would say. Like they had a right to tell her her own story. Like somehow they knew what was going on.

She grew so angry at the world. and that girl, once afraid of nothing, became afraid of herself. Afraid of love. Afraid of the nightmares if she went to sleep, and afraid of what the sun would bring when it rose.

But don't fear, this is not a tragedy.

The father fell in love again. He grew softer. And the storm inside him came out less regularly. When his girlfriend was around he pretended like nothing had ever happened. That they were crazy to think it did. And that was ok, temporarily. Because it meant the bruises that tickled their skin from the inside could finally start to heal. And the broken siblings found a sanctuary in each other because they were the only ones that still remembered what had happened. The only ones that ever would.

And one day someone started saying the word forgiveness like it was an obligation. But the scars and the thorns pricked them, itching at them to never forget. And so they wove walls out of the rubble. Creating a blockade around their hearts to make sure it was not easy for him to get back in, or anyone for that matter.

And they grew up like flowers and vines twisting into each other. It was a miracle, but together they created a garden, a home. And each season a few more wildflowers sprouted from the weeds. And the color slowly came back.

And the girl, once so excited about life—

learned how to smile again.

You got kinder over time,
and now I would say we're almost friends.
But even all these years later,
I cannot ignore the fact
that you caused me so much pain,
and never cared enough to remember it.

One thing you didn't take from me was hope.
Sometimes I wish you had,
because I always think this time will be different,
that this time you'll care,
and each time it hurts when you don't.

Maybe it's my fault
for running at the same brick wall
over and over,
and expecting it to suddenly
turn to sand.

Growing up I learned that
it was ok for you to call me
a "bitch" and
an "asshole" and
a "fucking pig"
because you were angry.

But when I said it back,
I was no longer welcome in your house.
Because rage is only attractive when it's in poetry,
and if it's not attractive, it doesn't belong on a woman.

I was taught to apologize and ask permission.
That my desires were inconveniences,
and my voice was a sports car—
more valuable the quieter it was.

All I wanted to do was scream.
But you taught me that women don't yell, they cry,
so I learned to drown my anger in tears,
because a flood is better than a wildfire.

I don't think you understand
that these are the lessons you left me with.

I don't think you understand
that you were even a teacher in the first place.

You have always been able to
manipulate my heart in such a way
that even though I'm the one bleeding,
I offer you the very bandaids
that are holding me together.

Why does everyone leave?
Why do people,
and love,
and best friends
come and go like the wind?

Why does everyone decide I'm no longer enough
after I give them everything I have?

Why can't some people come,
and just for once—
stay?

Learning how to stand up for yourself is just shy of impossible
when you've been told all your life
that your silence is more valuable than your voice;
when you have had to earn the right to exist as yourself;
when you had to turn to writing
because you were never allowed to say what you really meant.

Learning how to stand up for yourself is scary
when friends have left you
because you finally opened your mouth;
when people have told you
you're taking up too much space in this universe;
when you've been bullied
because of how much light you were holding;
when it's been ingrained in you to wonder
if you're just being crazy—
if it really is all your fault like they say it is.

Learning how to stand up for yourself is a process.
It is a slow climb to what you deserve.
I envy the ones who have perfected it,
who don't let others ration their silence,
who don't fold when they are uncomfortable,
who don't allow people to guilt them into apologizing
for being *broken*.

I have allowed betrayers to sharpen their knife in front of me.
And far too many times,
I have watched quietly,
all the way up until the moment they stab me in the back.

And even then,
as they wipe the blood off their hands,
and walk away,
my trauma strangles all the words I want to scream
into bitter nothings
that never make it past my tongue.

I've grown to enjoy solitude.
It doesn't feel as lonely when you're accompanied
by a pen and some paper.

It gives me chills
the way the world trembles
when the past
is on it's way back.

Some people won't ever change.
Some people can't.
Consider yourself warned,
because it is the most draining kind of life
to believe that if you just love hard enough
you can transform someone
that is not willing to change their ways
into who you want them to be.

Believe me, I've tried.

Thoughts are just visitors
passing through our minds.
Sometimes they stay a while—
uninvited.

-Anxiety

I learned to lock my heart
the way I lock doors at night—
with the impending fear
that someone may try to break in.

They used to say it was cool that I had two houses.

They had no idea what I would have traded
to have two parents that loved each other.

To have one place I could plant my feet
and just be,
for more than an instant.

To not be caught in between two winds
with no say in which direction I'd get pulled.

I'll never understand how you poured oceans on me
but didn't notice me drowning.
What did you think I would make of the flood?
You can't expect someone to fly
when you've stood over them their whole life
drenching their wings.

People are meant to come and go in your life.
Some will stick around for a decade or two,
others, just for a moment—
to love you,
to break you,
to teach you.

Each person makes up a little piece of your story,
but very few are there for your entire journey.

And as I've let go of people
who promised me forever,
I've learned that maybe that's for the best.

I never meant to cause anyone pain,
and I like to think the people that have hurt me
didn't mean to either.

But it doesn't change the fact
that I have a list of people
I will never take beneath my surface again
because I am still trying to repair the damage they did
last time I gave them access to my heart.

It doesn't change the fact
that there are people I share blood with
that missed years of my life
because they didn't care enough to show up
when I needed them the most.

I like to think they didn't mean to hurt me,
but it doesn't change the fact that they did.

I think of you far more than I want to,
the words you left me with feel bitter in the silence.
I can't escape the regret
that I gave so much of my heart
to someone that never planned on sticking around.
That didn't respect me enough to tell me the truth,
or have the grace to say goodbye.

I wonder if you understand how much you hurt me.
If I understand how much I hurt you.
Perhaps that's all we will remember about each other—
how things could have been so different
if we had just sat down and had one of those
long conversations that made everything better,
if we hadn't waited so long to say what we really meant.

It hurts less to believe
that our friendship fell apart for a reason,
and not a mere miscommunication.
But I want you to know that I've scattered poems
all across this world.

So if you ever wonder about an old friend,
you could easily see
that despite all my anger—
I really just *miss you.*

My worst enemy has always been myself.

I have wars that churn inside me
and worlds I'm constantly building and tearing down.

This cycle leaves me in tired pieces most nights.
But that doesn't stop all the parts of me
from fighting against each other,

because that's more familiar
than feeling *peace*.

He rejected his own daughter,
because he saw in her,
all the parts of himself he was too afraid to be.

He convinced her that she was unworthy of love,
because he was so unhappy in his own skin,
so terrified to wipe the dust off his wings.

He pulled her down like a weight,
because he couldn't stand

to watch her fly.

Poetry brings me home,
to a part of myself that is just for me.

I've come to realize that people who are cruel,
people that don't know how to love,
simply lost track of their key,
and can't find their way home.

—How torturing that must be.

Moon cycle after moon cycle
I practiced the art of smiling to others
when I was crying inside,
and became a master at saying I was ok when I wasn't.

I didn't let anyone see
that inside I was trapped
in the deepest part
of the darkest ocean.
That while yes, I could catch glimpses of light
every once in a while,
the surface was so far away.

I don't know if I'll ever be able
to swim the way I used to—
careless and free.

Because after hitting rock bottom,
it's hard to even imagine
dipping my toes in the water ever again.

Sister,
Do not let the city lights swallow you whole.
Do not forget what silence smells like,
or the way the wind feels different
when you're on top of a mountain.

When they realize you sing like an angel,
and they ask for your autograph,
don't forget about us —
and this small town
you so desperately ran from.

Sometimes it's ok to sit in your pain.
To hold it tightly to your heart
and keep it warm instead of pushing it away.

Sometimes it's ok to take a break
from the inspirational quotes
and the people telling you it will all work out.

Sometimes it's ok to not try and fix everything;
to let it fall apart and sit in the crumbles for a moment
before rushing to put it all back together.

Sometimes going to sleep
and waking up the next day—
is *plenty*.

Darling,
I know what you are going through right now.
I know the way you lie awake at night
hoping for someone to come in and see that you are crying,
longing for someone to notice.
I see right through that smile—
the one you show others so they won't ask.
I only know this because I lived it too.
The tears only come when you're alone.
You spend your whole day giving everyone else your love
and leave none for yourself, I know.

Darling,
You don't have to keep trying to forgive yourself
for something you never did.
I know that standing up for yourself is not easy,
that it doesn't make you feel empowered - not yet.
It makes you feel small
and fills you with the guilt of a thousand wars.
I know the way those conversations linger in your head.
That you can't find any peace, even when you're asleep.

If I could travel back in time and hug you, I would.
I would give you all the warmth the blankets couldn't.
I would give you permission to ask for help,
permission to realize that you were doing
what was best for you.
I would tell you that's it's ok to put yourself before others.

But if you were resting, I would not wake you up,
I wouldn't dare disturb that peace.
Because darling, I know that the worst part of your day
is trying to fall asleep.

Writing saved my life—
when it all became too much
I poured the pain out into poetry.
I let the paper absorb everything
I'd been holding in for years.

I could feel my shoulders soften,
I could feel myself letting go.

And only then did I start to *heal.*

I come as a full course meal.
I will no longer hand myself out like a menu
and wait for people to pick and choose.

The only thing harder than learning,
is unlearning all the lessons and biases
you handed to me like fruit to munch on,
a never ending bowl.
It's hard to realize
that what you've been eating your whole life is
poison.

Ignorance is no longer bliss.
Ignorance is gasoline on a flame,
and I will no longer sit back and allow people
to pretend they don't understand
that the world is burning.

America,
I used to think you were the greatest place in the world.
But lately I have grown uncomfortable
with the way your name tastes in my mouth.
You preach liberty and justice for all,
but you have given people permission to dehumanize others
and call it patriotism.

—We could be so much better than this.

I can't walk along the plains of my country
without a million souls crunching beneath my feet.
Without the gunshots of hate
piercing through this "one nation undivided".

In school they teach us that once we had a civil war.

I don't think it's over yet.

If you knew someone you loved was dying
would you throw salt on the wound?
Turn a blind eye?

In the face of great loss
humans have the incredible strength
to make the impossible happen.

So why do we treat mother earth so cruelly
as she begins to die in front of us?

The eyes of future generations are on us,
the fate of our species is upon us,
and I've had enough of everyone pretending
that someone else is going to come along and fix it—
that we have enough time to put it off until tomorrow.

I'm tired of pretending that our grandchildren won't
look at us and ask, "why?"
Why did we take this magical place
and treat her so selfishly?
That it won't break our hearts
when we finally see what we have done.

—We only get one chance.

They tell us we are young.
That protesting won't change laws.
They don't understand
that if we don't,
we have everything to lose.

We fell in love right there in history class
with the idea of all we could be.
My teacher saw us,
he saw into our souls
and was able to draw out the best pieces
that we all kept hidden.

He taught us the world's history from evolution to now
and everything in between that he could pack into one year,
and we all listened,
because he made us care.

He never quizzed us on a date
or asked us to memorize anyone's name—
instead he had us look deep inside ourselves
to find the history of the world written on our bones.

To reflect on our past
and decide who we wanted to be,
which qualities of our fallen heroes
we wanted to grow in ourselves.
Which morals from every culture we wanted to believe.

He invited us to dream up our future
through reflection of the past.
But mostly, he inspired us to live in the present,
and changed our lives by showing us
that there is always a safe space in this world
within ourselves.

I never lived by the ocean,
maybe that's why I write so obsessively about it.
Because to me being near the waves
feels like being alive.

Like a vast infinity of ups and downs—
terrifying,
invigorating,
extraordinary,
all at the same time.

Why is it that you are so afraid to go take what you want,
to grab it without any uncertainty
and to know in your heart of hearts that you deserve it?

Why do you wait for someone to offer,
stroll up to your desires and ask politely?
Why do you question so often if you are worthy?

Why do you nibble at life,
when you have every chance to
devour?

There are castles everywhere
filled to the brim with stories
swallowed by the wind
and long *forgotten*.

Most nights I lay awake dreaming
of leaving everything behind
except my passport and a journal.

Floating from city to city,
staying only long enough to not be forgotten,
disappearing to the next adventure
just before finishing the last,
reviving my soul at each stop.

There are so many places I've never been,
full of people I have so much space for
in my heart already,
even though their presence is no more than an idea.

I can't wait to to collect memories
from every corner of the earth,
to splash in the vastness of this beautiful world.

I've spent years in the lost and found,
and while coming home is the warmest feeling—
I will never get tired of getting lost.
Not in bookstores,
not on city streets,
and definitely not in myself.

It's ok if you've changed.
It's ok if you're not who you expected you'd be,
if you didn't do everything you wanted to.
It's ok to outgrow people,
and leave things behind.
It's ok to move on from something
that was once your everything.

It's ok if you're different now.

You stood there,
intertwined with the flowers,
like you were one of them.

You stood there,
softly breathing golden light onto their petals,
like a magician playing tricks on the stars—
a never ending harmony of "hallelujah".

They needed you,
like a sailor needs her compass home.

You are on your way, baby.
Keep shining.

Until the dirt and the weeds
prick your legs
and fill your socks;
until your hair gets tangled
and your cheeks numb
from the way the wind feels
out of a moving car window;
until your legs ache from running
and your neck hurts
from looking up at the stars;
chase that feeling—
of being
electric.

On my most dreary days—
hand me a map of Europe
and a cup of tea,
and just wait
for my dreams
to encapsulate
my soul.

She said taking a good photograph
was like catching the wind or the waves,
like seeing into another realm.

That an artist can capture time itself—
and save it for later.

While climbing your most laborious mountain,
the world may seem dark.
But I am here to remind you that, darling,
you are the sun.

I swear she's done this whole life thing before.
She belongs to an old soul
and breathes love instead of air.
I am so lucky to be a part of her world,
to be a contact in her phone.
Her beauty radiates,
but she is so much more than her silhouette.
She is the goddess of the sun
and the keeper of the stars,
the trees dance when she looks their way
and the sunsets are always trying to impress her.
She doesn't know this, but I do.
I wish she would look in the mirror
and see what I see—
that she is a wildflower,
and the way she doesn't apologize
for being different
has always been what makes her *beautiful.*

She is broken;
you must ask before you touch her.
She will not tell you this.
When she says she's fine, she's not;
you must love her anyway.

Learn to read her eyes,
and do not allow her to apologize when they fill with tears.
The amount of oceans that will pour from them
may surprise you,
she did not choose to be this way.

Show her that she is not a mistake that needs to be fixed,
show her that she is beautiful
because of the way she cares too much about people;
for the way she gives without any expectation of return.

Do not take advantage of her love.
She will always put others needs before her own,
so be careful not to drain all her love away,
or she will have none left for herself.

The first thing I noticed was
how her spirit made me want to get drunk on life.
Our friendship has always tasted like adventure—
skinny dipping under the summer moon,
and laughing so hard we could probably wake up the sun.

It's so easy to get lost with her—
in poetry sections of bookstores and deep conversations.
You should see the way our voices become one
as music pours out of the car windows
like rum on her breath.
She's the beat of every song,
the life of every party,
the kind of friend that sees you
when you're hiding from yourself.
And some of my favorite memories in life
are turning empty streets into dance floors
and watching her red curls bounce
as she twirls like a wildflower in the breeze.

I wonder if she understands how different she is
from any other friends I've had,
if she recognizes how many of my poems
are about the way our souls intertwine,
if she'll ever understand how much I love her.

She noticed that I had been holding my breath
for so long,
and finally gave me permission
to *breathe*.

Sometimes it takes disaster and great tragedy
to move forward.
Sometimes a setback is the only way to advance.

Out of the black death came the renaissance,
out of the crumbles came a revolution
of artists and exploration.
All you need is one person
to spark a brilliant fire
and change everything.

And one thing I've learned from history
is that they are always,
always
the people you least expect.

When I was a child, people used to ask me
if I could have one superpower,
what would it be?
Many of the other kids would giggle
and hold out their arms like wings,
"to fly," they would say,
and leap into the air hoping for once
that the ground wouldn't hit them on the way down.

But there was a different impossibility
that intrigued me far more—
to know every language that existed.
There is no better superpower, I thought,
than the ability to connect with every human in the world.
To have no limitations of who could be a friend,
to be able to speak to anyone
with more than just my eyes.

The very essence of being alive is poetry.
Each step is a stanza,
each line a promise
that we will never stop writing,
we will never stop living.

That the end of this book
is simply the *beginning* of the next one.

She left all she knew for an adventure to find herself.
5,270 miles west, she came to the United States of America
because somehow she knew that all the strength she didn't have yet
was waiting there for her.
Beautiful and brave, like a warrior,
she stood out in a field, like a wildflower.
She saw the light in everything
and was the kind of person that made people smile for no reason.

She tried to swallow up every bit of America she could:
learn every word, meet every person, make every memory.
And even though she smiled most of the time,
for 320 nights when she lay down on a bed that wasn't hers,
she would dream of her home, and the people she left behind.
She would imagine on repeat
the moment when she would see them again,
and counted down the days.
And we all understood why she would cry,
but maybe none of us truly understood.
Because none of us were brave enough
to leave everything we knew behind.
So we listened to her talk about her country,
and her life in Madrid like it was her favorite movie,
and we loved it because it meant we got to spend time with her.

And one day, when she lays down on her own bed
after having Tapas and Nestea with her family,
she will dream of us,
and the way we found home in each other that year.
She will remember the few basketball games we won,
and belting Tequila by Dan and Shay on top of the mountains.
About how we'd talk about our futures and our fears in gym class,
and how we gave each other every part of ourselves.
She will remember how we tried with every string in our bodies
to make the time slow down.

But mostly she'll remember having to learn
that she will forever be stuck between two worlds,
missing one or the other.
Because there are too many people,
from too many cities,
too far away,
that love her too much.

That no matter where she goes,
or who she's missing,
she will always be home.

The rhythm of our heartbeats
is my favorite song.
All I want to do
is *dance*
to each other's existence.

"Carpe Diem,"
they screamed from the rooftops
of the homes they built inside themselves.
"Now is our time.
You cannot hold us back anymore,
we are free."

Then the light came, and swept me off my feet.

Some things can't be explained,
not even with poetry.
But I still keep trying to make sense of
everything,
even when I know
that the very beauty
lies in its mystery.

They were lost in each other's eyes,
so caught in the magic of it all.
Because that's really what falling in love is—
Magic.

You are the kind of book I can't put down.
All I want to do is keep flipping your pages.
I want to read every chapter if you'll let me,
I want to understand all that is you.

And when I get to the end of this book in my hands,
I want to help you keep writing it.
But this time, I want to be a character in your story.
I want my name to appear in ink on these pages,
I want you to let me in on this beautiful life of yours.

I'm sorry I didn't tell you I loved you
when I knew I did.
I guess those words have been used against me
so many times,
by people who always seem to leave,
that it scares me to say them out loud,
because I really want you to be different.

The moonlight danced
on the water under the stars,
and the birds practiced their songs quietly,
and the flowers slept
from a long day of growing,
and the air smelled like
a brand new morning on its way,
and the trees smiled
because they were alive,
and in that moment—
everything was *ok*.

Won't you let me sail the waves with you?
We can dive into the darkest depths of each other.

And if you ever feel like drowning,
I promise I will be there
to bring you back to solid ground.

I fell in love to his sweet smile
and soft brown eyes.
To the constant adventure
of trying new things together.

To exploring the world
and each other's minds.
To the music,
and our twisting bodies
discovering every way to fit together.
To the vibration of his heartbeat,
and the warmth of his body against mine.

To the light of the moon,
and the normal between every extraordinary moment.
To the sound of " *I'll never forget you.* "

Some of us are made for antique stores.
Because the way an old typewriter
or record player
leaves dust on our hands,
reminds us,
that we come from
the cracked music
and half written poems
of all the people
who have ever found peace
in the idea that *souls never die.*

I told her I was scared for him to leave,
scared to have my heart broken.
She looked at me with warm eyes and smiled,
"It's like watching a sunset," she said,
"You know it's going to go away—
but if you don't watch it
just because it's going to end,
you miss the whole thing,
and it's really a shame
because sunsets are
extraordinary."

I started missing him before he was even gone.
Crazy how someone can be standing right in front of you,

and feel thousands of miles away.

Sitting watching the sunset
she was thinking about him,
the way she always did
when she saw something *beautiful.*

He came here for a good story,
to leave the city air that was suffocating his adventure.
He came here to meet new people,
and to remember what it felt like to breathe.
And she was waiting,
for someone new, for someone wonderful and different.
And one day he showed up,
and the fall leaves and cold air whispered to them
that it was each other they had been looking for.

But the boy had a plane ticket home.
He was only ever meant to be a pop up traveling show,
he was not there to stay.
And still, the girl gave him her heart,
knowing that he would be the most loving person
to experience magic for the first time with,
and that time would never be wasted, for they had none to spare.

She knew that the end would come with the blink of an eye.
That walking away from a relationship both of them wanted to be in,
would tear her apart.
That not being able to talk to him
or see his face
or be in the same hemisphere
or look at the same stars—
would be excruciating.

That on that last day he would hand most of her heart back to her,
keeping a little for himself until the day he dies.
And that when that plane flew into the stars,
across seasons and through time,
the girl would look down at the pieces of her heart in her hands
and smile—
Because it is better to have loved and lost,
than to have never loved at all.

How do you find the words to say goodbye forever
to someone you don't want to stop loving?

How do you find the music within yourself
to dance to the song that created your relationship
one last time?

How do you hold someone tight enough
during that last hug,
knowing you may never be able
to press your heart against theirs again?

How do you let them go,
when every cell in your body
wants them to stay?

To the woman I was before my first heartbreak:
I see you.
I know you are scared,
anticipating the end
as you feel it approaching—
love does a good job of keeping you up at night
when it's dying.

I know it seems like without him
nothing will go on,
that your heart may break so badly,
it could stop beating altogether.

But just remember,
a phoenix can only bloom
from the ashes.

—I promise you will be ok.

Tonight, the moon's arc was so smooth,
she was lying on her back
looking so relaxed.
I was sitting out in the cold,
gravity pulling my feet to the hard ground,
but meeting her gaze warmed me up,
the way beautiful things do.
And in that moment all I wanted
was a secondhand pair of wings,
nothing fancy or expensive,
just something to get me close enough to reach her touch,
to climb up to her and rest.
To take a break from this whole earth thing,
just for the night.

We left pieces of ourselves in each other.
No matter how hard I try to forget,
you will always be a part of me.

Distance took our sweet, sweet love,
and stretched it out until there was no more taste.
There was no getting around your plane ticket home,
no amount of love can stop time,
but man, did we try.
Such a shame that you had to go at the best part,
when we were so helplessly falling in love with life
and so willingly sharing that love with each other.
Such a tragedy that eight months
was all that was in the cards for us.
I like to think that more time
would have only made us better,
but distance stretched us out,
and time urged us to forget and move on.
Because sometimes good things lose all their sweet taste
when you hold them in your mouth for too long—
and I guess you and I
were not made for that kind of love story.
I guess some adventures are best left at the climax,
that way they never have a chance to turn *bitter*.

The day he got on that plane,
I forgot how to breathe.

My lungs could not grasp enough air
through the tears streaming down my face,
my heart wouldn't stop burning for long enough
to remember how to press the gas on my car.

When there was nothing left to do
but drive away,
my heart, my body, my soul
were screaming at me not to go,
not to say goodbye to the greatest love I'd ever felt,
not to leave his touch forever.

And when the tear stains finally dried,
and his smell slowly drifted from my memory,
I understood why my body had frozen at the wheel.
It wanted me to stay for one more moment,
because it knew that watching his face disappear
in my rear view mirror,
would feel like getting stabbed right through my chest,
that the agony would linger for weeks, months,
that all I would wish for in those coming sleepless nights,

was one more moment,
before all the *pain*.

Too much steadiness makes me uneasy.
At least feeling something means I'm alive,
at least feeling heartbreak
means I loved.

Loving someone
who is far away and out of reach,
someone who isn't coming back—
is like a cloud that lingers over your bed at night,
threatening to start pouring rain if you
make the slightest move.
A cloud that ruins every sunset because you don't get to
share the beauty with them.
It manifests so far into you pretending to be ok,
that months go by
and you still grab at sheets and pillows
because it's something to hold.
And one day the cloud disappears,
but only because you are so used to it now
it has become a part of you.
No one can see it anymore so no one asks.
They mistake your smile for progress,
and congratulate you.
As if the fact that your pain is invisible now
should be celebrated.
And in some strange way
all you want is to hold onto the way your heart burns,
because it's better than not feeling them at all.
And even though the rain doesn't come as often anymore,
the darkness still blocks the sun.

I wonder if you are looking at the moon
in this same moment;
if you even remember
what the moon once meant to us.

Take me to the beaches,
to the coast,
to the waves.
Take me somewhere that is not here,
because here you are everywhere.

And I can't heal
if every time I go out, or come home
you are there,
reminding me
that you are *gone.*

Often all we can do is breathe,
and even that can be hard sometimes.

Dear me,
I love you the most
when you are being yourself.

Today I drove up to that spot with the view,
the one with the lights we used to dance underneath.
I spent a little time with myself,
she and I are becoming much better friends lately.
We've grown closer since you left.

Loving you was the luckiest mistake I ever made—
we fell quick and hard,
the epitome of a great song.
But loving myself is different,
and I have a feeling this love will last much longer.

We used to run out at low tide and collect hermit crabs.
Funny how even as kids,
we knew that their home was inside their shell—
not the patch of sand we found them in.

It took me over a decade
to realize that humans are exactly the same.
Home is inside us,

always,

even if we swim far away.

I spend a lot of time in my skin
feeling critical, displeased;
wasting time not loving myself.
But this body of mine is so much more
than the outermost layer that everyone can see.
And on the days I look in the mirror
and don't like what I perceive,
I must remind myself that there is so much I'm missing.

That this body represents a cosmic journey
of evolution and revolution.
That this skin has bled,
and bruised,
and ached,
and healed.
These dripping palms that are always reaching for more,
have led me to everyone I've ever loved.
This brain of mine can assemble ideas,
can brew words into poetry.
That this smile is a passage to the world,
my peace offering.
That these ears can create music in the moans
of a body well celebrated by its soul.

I must remind myself that
this heart can break,
and break,
and break,
and keep on loving—
and what deserves love more than that?

We lock away our secrets
and push them deep down
so they feel farther away,
but they will always be inside us,
no matter how well we hide the key.

I have stared into the souls of many ceilings,
and memorized the tiles on countless bathroom floors.
I've spent days of my life
contemplating ways I could make others more comfortable
with all the love I was holding.

But I have learned
that if society can't appreciate my colors,
if they're more comfortable with black and white,
that is their place of shame,
not mine.

We search and search
for things we won't find,
we wait for satisfaction
to appear on our doorstep,
we strive for perfection,
but we are constantly letting ourselves down,
because we will never have enough.

Or maybe we've had everything all along,
we've just been looking in all the wrong places.
Maybe we sailed across oceans to find happiness,
but forgot to look in the boat.

—Everything you will ever need is inside you.

There is nothing more sad
than the death of a stargazer
with dreams still tucked inside them,
untouched.

We are all on the same team,
just looking at life from different angles:
The dreamers and the realists,
the explorers and the homebodies,
the spirituals and the scientists,
the mathematicians and the artists—
we are all just seeking to understand.

And although we probably never will,
life is so much richer if you are trying.

We all start as a seed,
no bigger than a thought.
We don't get a say in which garden we are planted in
or if we are nurtured correctly,
but once our roots are planted
and our minds can breathe for themselves,
we have a choice—
In which direction our branches grow,
in how we spread our leaves,
if we choose to be strong or tall,
beautiful or real,
in what we leave behind.
We get to choose if we want to clean the air
or make it harder for everyone to breathe,
if we want to suffocate the freedom out of others,
or love with everything we've got.
If we want to dance with the wind,
or let it blow us away.

But we have a choice.
We always have a choice.

There are two sides to every story.
This is not poetry,
it is truth,
and I hope with all my heart
that you never forget this.

Never be so married to your rightness,
that you become blind to the other side,
and there is always another side,
because the moment you stop seeking
to understand,
is the moment you stop growing.

Some people leave when there is
nothing left to be learned from them,
sometimes the greatest lesson they give you,
is in the *goodbye*.

When a star dies,
no one hears it explode.
We simply see the light go dim
moments after it has caved in upon its own soul,
and burst into a million suns—
spreading all that it has witnessed into the universe
to disappear,
until it is ready to be *found*.

There are certain days that change your life forever.
And each year when those dates come,
the whole world feels weird;
a mix between a dream and how it was before.
I have a few dates that will always be hard
no matter how old I get.
Today is one of them;
you were on the cusp of death all night,
and when I woke up,
you were gone.

I remember the shock.
Dropping to my knees and completely surrendering
to whatever took you away from my world.
For three years I sat in anxiety of that moment.
Every time my mother said there was bad news,
or that she had something to tell us,
every birthday wish and 11:11,
every shooting star,
it was all a desperate cry for more time,
just a little more time.

When you died, I could not imagine a world without you,
it felt so empty and bland.
But now it is "normal",
and my heart no longer stops
when someone says your name.

But to me fall is not just the dying of leaves,
it is a reminder of the end,
it is the season of the wind
taking you away.

I have gone through my life
trying to do the best I can,
just like anyone else.

But I have hurt people along the way;
I know that.
And in turn, I've been hurt by many people.

I have been on the wrong end of many battles,
fought when I should have surrendered,
and surrendered when I should have fought.

Part of growing up is getting it all wrong.
But learning from your mistakes
shows a lot more about your character,
than the fact that you made them in the first place.

I hope that when I die,
in all the crumbled up memories of my life
scattered across the world,
what I've left behind
is nothing but love.

I hope that somehow people remember who I was,
and not who they wanted me to be.
That I have contributed a worthwhile verse
to this magnificent song,
this universal harmony.

I hope that I die in peace.
That I have a moment to detach
and say goodbye to myself,
before nature comes with her rigid hands,
to take me home—
back to the earth,
to the sky,
and the stars.

If I call you now,
it rings and rings and rings in my ear,
like the last words I ever said to you.
Eventually it tells me that you are unreachable,
that your mailbox is full.
That I can send you a message
but you won't ever hear it.

I still have moments, all these years later
where I long to call you,
to tell you that I haven't forgotten.
That even as I grow older,
and learn that you were not the man I remember you as,
I still love you.
I still miss you.

I wonder where you are right now,
where your memories are floating,
where your soul is dreaming.
If only I could call you.
If only you weren't impossibly far away.

Whenever I hear that song,
from now until the day I join you wherever you are,
I will sway the way we did under the moon,
and remember the way you taught me to love—
To love myself,
to love others,
and to love the people I hated.

Because you knew I would miss out on so much,
if I ever forgot *how to love*.

Your photos and dead funeral flowers decorate my room,
bittersweet memories of a life well lived.
Every day I am reminded of you,
of how you inspired me to start writing poetry
because somehow you knew it would save me,
when you couldn't anymore.

When the pulse fades from my body,
and my soul goes to wherever souls go,
I want you to know,
that loving you,
was one of the greatest gifts of my life.

We have all been on journeys
for billions of years to get here,
right here,
right now.

As a result of cosmic perfection
you are exactly where you are meant to be.

Once upon a time,
we were all a part of the stars.

These shells for our souls
were once stardust,
were once balls of embers and flames.
We were literally made from light.

But there is darkness in the universe too,
burried inside each one of us—
everywhere you look you will find both.

But one thing I've learned
from all the star people I've met,
is that it is up to each one of us
to choose what we want to see.

You were my deepest pain,
and angriest poems.
You were the reason I cried myself to sleep for months,
and you made me want to give up
again and again.

But I need to thank you for the hardship,
because with that
you handed me,
my greatest strength.

Sit in your skin for a moment;
feel what it's like to look through your eyes.
Pay attention to the way music vibrates
through your whole body.
Savor the way thoughts can drift right through your mind.
Taste something sweet
and hold it in your mouth for too long.
Allow your soul to float around in your skin.

Embrace the feeling of being you.
you are existing—
and that is *extraordinary.*

We talked a lot about death in those last months.
But mostly, we talked about life,
and sitting in a chemotherapy office
after three years of fighting cancer,
he told me something that changed my life.

"You don't get to choose how you die," he said,
"but you do get to choose how you live,
and I hope you choose to *live it up*."

Piece by piece,
we rebuild the moon each night.
With our words, we pull the tides closer to our chests,
swallow the pain and turn it into art.
We take the once unconquerable mountains
crumbling around us
and make them glow.

We spend our nights tripping over ourselves,
on everything we always wanted to say,
because what is all of this for
if we don't get to make some noise?
If we don't leave something worth remembering behind,
even if it's just in the subtle way the moon smiles?

We bring life to the remains,
and sprinkle beginnings
in the pockets of everyone we meet—
because there is no point in feeling truth,
if there is not magic scattered
among every corner of the sky
and every speck of the ground.

And no one can create beauty out of dirt and rock
better than us.

Tomorrow will bring waves
just like today and every day before.
The only constant
is in the way the ups and downs never end.

But one thing I do know,
one thing I've always known,
is that you are the light—

never stop being the light.

The Beginning—

Acknowledgments

First I want to thank *you*, whoever you are, for reading this book— you are making my dreams come true.

To the poetry community on Instagram— I will forever be grateful for the friendships I've made and support I've received from you all.

To the Fab 5— for keeping me grounded and encouraging me to fly. My love for you is beyond anything words can describe.

To Nana— for financially supporting this project and for being the first person to believe in my poetry. I couldn't have done this without you.

To Pa— for inspiring me to write this book, although you will never get to read it. I promise I will always live it up.

To Lucia— for giving me the tools to understand the waves. Your guidance and friendship has changed my life.

To my friends and mentors— for supporting me throughout this whole journey. I have learned what's most important in life from you all.

Lastly, to my family— the one I was born into and the ones I have found along the way.

Thank you all from the bottom of my heart.

Follow @poetry.by.Julia on Instagram
to continue riding the waves with me.

CPSIA information can be obtained
at www.ICGtesting.com
Printed in the USA
LVHW081134120621
690063LV00013B/2026